# Venus

## by J.P. Bloom

ABDO
PLANETS
Kids

**abdopublishing.com**

Published by Abdo Kids, a division of ABDO, PO Box 398166, Minneapolis, Minnesota 55439.

Copyright © 2015 by Abdo Consulting Group, Inc. International copyrights reserved in all countries. No part of this book may be reproduced in any form without written permission from the publisher.

Printed in the United States of America, North Mankato, Minnesota.

102014

012015

THIS BOOK CONTAINS
RECYCLED MATERIALS

Photo Credits: iStock, NASA, Science Source, Shutterstock, Thinkstock

Production Contributors: Teddy Borth, Jennie Forsberg, Grace Hansen

Design Contributors: Laura Rask, Dorothy Toth


Library of Congress Control Number: 2014943720

Cataloging-in-Publication Data

J.P. Bloom.

 Venus / J.P. Bloom.

   p. cm. -- (Planets)

ISBN 978-1-62970-722-8 (lib. bdg.)

Includes index.

1. Venus (Planet)--Juvenile literature.  2. Solar system--Juvenile literature.  I. Title.

523.42--dc23

        2014943720

# Table of Contents

## Venus

Venus is a **planet**. Planets **orbit** stars. Planets in our solar system orbit the sun.

4

Venus is the second-closest

**planet** to the sun. It is about

67 million miles (108 million km)

away from the sun.

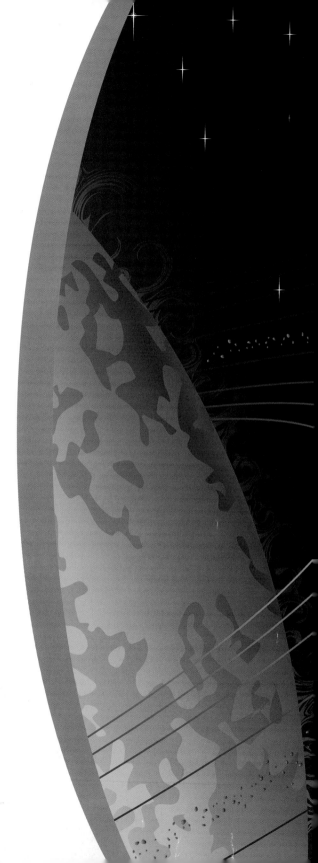

Venus

Mercury

Earth

Mars

Jupiter

Saturn

Uranus

Neptune

7

Venus fully **orbits** the sun every 225 days. One year on Venus is 225 days on Earth.

Venus

The Sun

Venus spins while in **orbit**.

The spin makes day and night.

One full spin takes about 243

Earth days.

# Earth
## 7,918 miles
## (12,743 km)

# Venus
## 7,520 miles
## (12,102 km)

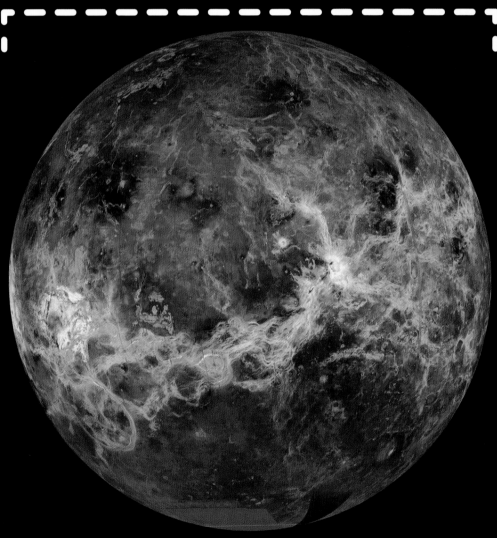

11

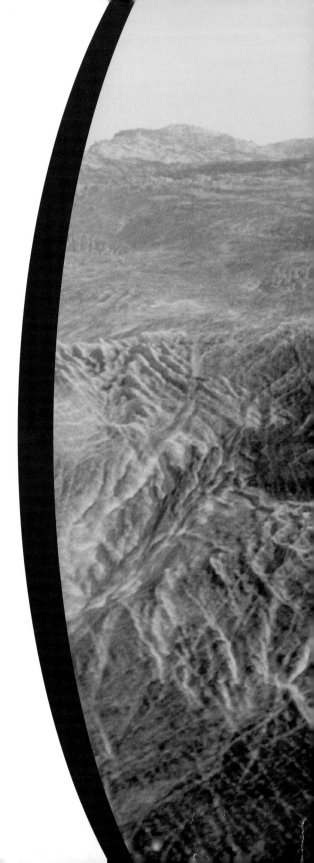

Venus has thick air.

The air traps heat.

13

## Hottest Planet

Venus is the hottest **planet** in our solar system. Temperatures on Venus can reach 870°F (466°C).

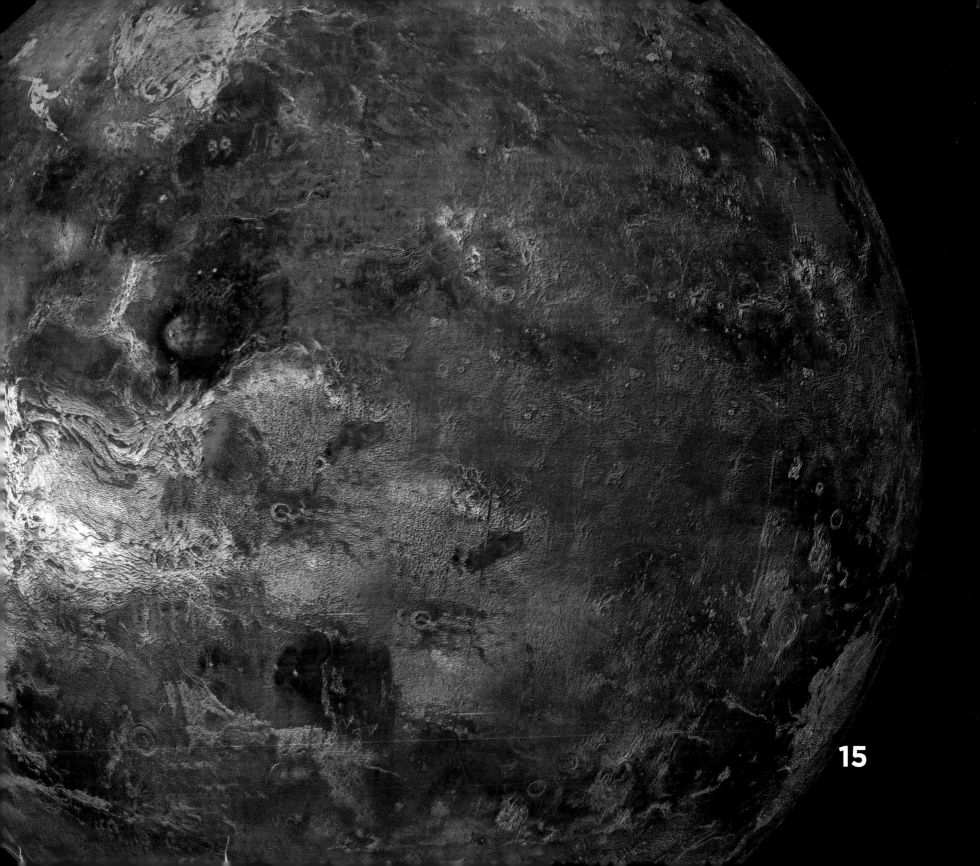

15

## Volcanoes

Venus has many **volcanoes**.

Other parts of Venus are flat

and smooth.

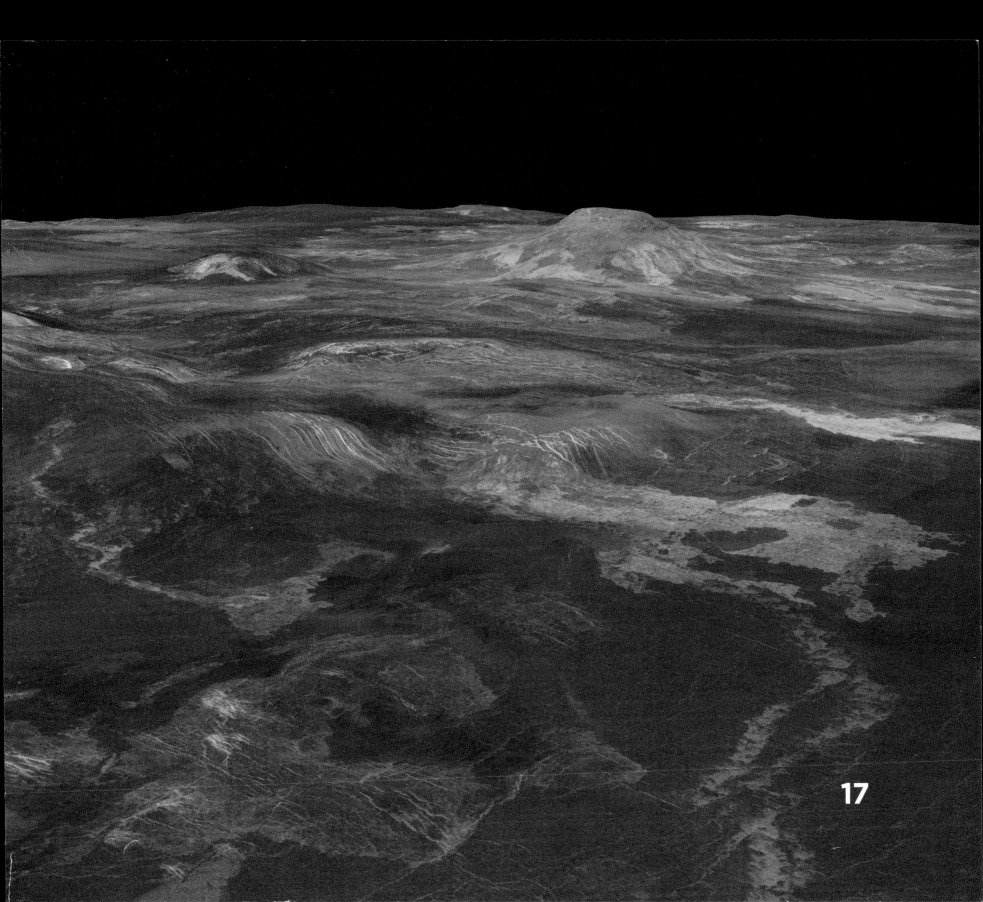

17

## Clouds

Venus has clouds. The top layer of clouds move about 224 mph (360 kph). This is fast for how slow Venus spins.

19

## Venus from Earth

Venus is brighter than any other **planet**. Its clouds **reflect** light. You can see Venus from Earth at night.

Venus - - - •

21

# More Facts

- Venus is very bright, like a star. It is sometimes called the "morning star" or the "evening star." Venus can be easily seen at those times.

- Venus is just a little bit smaller than Earth. The planets are not alike in many other ways.

- Venus spins in the opposite direction of most planets. Uranus is the only other planet to spin in the same direction as Venus. The sun rises in the west and sets in the east on Venus.

# Glossary

**orbit** – the path of a space object as it moves around another space object. To orbit is to follow its path.

**planet** – a large, round object in space (such as Earth) that travels around a star (such as the sun).

**reflect** – able to shine light back.

**volcano** – a large mountain or hill with a hole that can throw out lava, ash, and rock from beneath the Earth's crust.

# Index

## abdokids.com

Use this code to log on to abdokids.com and access crafts, games, videos, and more!

Abdo Kids Code:
PVK7228